Tame the Tiger

Negotiating from a position of power

Tame the Tiger

Negotiating from a position of power

Leonie McKeon

DoctorZed
Publishing
www.doctorzed.com

Books may be ordered through booksellers or by contacting:
www.leoniemckeon.com

ISBN: 978-0-6482118-9-1 (hc)
ISBN: 978-0-6481314-0-3 (sc)
ISBN: 978-0-6481314-1-0 (ebk)

A CiP number for this title can be found at the National Library of Australia.

Cover image © Trish Pollock

Printed in Australia, UK and USA.
rev. date 08/08/2017

Contents

Acknowledgements

When I started writing *The Dao of Negotiation*, I realised that although I am a Chinese expert, authoring a book required new skills. I would like to thank Nicole Turner for teaching me how to write a book. I would like to thank Jennifer McKeon who read and re-read the drafts so many times she might now be a 36 Strategies expert too. In particular I want to thank Shelley Rogers who encouraged and supported me to write *The Dao of Negotiation*. She also challenged me with essential questions like 'how' and 'why', and moved sentences around so my words made much more sense. And finally many thanks to Michaela Crisp for her wonderful research skills, and to everyone else behind the scenes who have made this book happen.

*"Appear weak when you are strong,
And strong when you are weak."*

Sun Tzu, *The Art of War*

Leonie's Journey

*M*y friend and I had been backpacking around the world for a year and a half when we started to run out of money. Luckily, we had just enough to buy a cheap airfare to Hong Kong where we thought there would be no difficulty getting a job. The plan was to replenish our funds and continue our journey. I managed to get only one interview, which was as a topless barmaid. The owner of the bar decided that I had neither the personality nor the body to be serving drinks in a G–string.

My travelling companion was sitting in the foyer of the club waiting for me while the owner conducted the interview. She asked me what I thought my friend could do, and without thinking I said he could be a bouncer at her club. She looked him over; although he stood more than six feet tall, he had lost so much weight in India his eyes were sunken. She advised us Hong Kong was no place for people of our ages with little money. I had just celebrated my 26th birthday in India, and despite feeling mature we were sent on our way feeling disappointed and rejected. On reflection, she had given us an excellent piece of advice.

That night we returned to our cheap, unhygienic hostel where we met an English backpacker in the corridor. He suggested we go to Taiwan and teach English, explaining that he had lived there for a year and left with a pocket full of money. I asked him where Taiwan was, demonstrating how little I knew about the geography of the region.

Off we went to Taiwan with no teaching experience and no more understanding of Chinese culture than we had gained at our favourite Chinese restaurant in Melbourne. I spent the next five years living in Taiwan, where I developed skills in English teaching that I would never have believed possible. During my first year, in order to get a job, I had to pretend I was American, because English schools in Taiwan only employed people from the United States of America and the Taiwanese wanted to learn to speak English with an American accent. Most places only accepted university graduates so I instantly became a university graduate, while the truth was I had only completed high school.

After five years of living in Taiwan, learning to speak Mandarin and to read traditional Chinese characters, I travelled through China for a year before returning to Australia to study, completing a bachelor's degree in Anthropology and a Graduate Diploma in Business Enterprise. On completion of my studies, I opened my own business 'Chinese Language and Cultural Advice', which provided cultural awareness and Mandarin language training to Australian businesses wanting to get into the Chinese market. I operated that business for fifteen years. In 2013, I sold the business, and I now work for several businesses as a China Strategist, designing and implementing their China strategy. I am also a conference speaker and a presenter delivering workshops on the 36 Strategies derived from Sun Tzu's *The Art of War*.

The Missing Piece

In Taiwan I studied Mandarin and learned to read, write and speak the language. Even though I lived in Taiwan, where I immersed myself as much as possible in Chinese culture and became competent in Mandarin Chinese, I still had the feeling there was a piece of information missing. There were gaps in my understanding of what was happening within my interactions in workplaces, negotiating purchases and communicating with my Chinese friends. Several years later, I discovered that the crucial piece missing in my knowledge was the understanding of the 36 Strategies.

These 36 Strategies are a set of ancient idioms derived from *The Art of War*. Many people are familiar with *The Art of War*, which is an ancient Chinese military text dating from the 5th Century BC. Supposedly written by the ancient Chinese military strategist known as Sun Tzu. *The Art of War* is considered a definitive work on military strategy and tactics and has had an influence on Eastern and Western military thinking, and business tactics. The 36 Strategies are thought to have originated as colloquial sayings that may have developed through similar sources to *The Art of War*. What is relevant is that in our contemporary world they are used daily in negotiation and communication interactions by most Chinese people.

Fifteen years ago when I was only a couple of years into my first Chinese-based business and on one of my regular trips to Shanghai, I was introduced to the 36 Strategies for the first time by a man whom I met at a networking function.

It was one of those chance meetings when someone passes through your life, and however brief the encounter, it has the power to change your view of the world. He invited me for coffee. At that time Starbucks was a popular meeting place for Westerners, being one of the few places in Shanghai to sell drinkable coffee. Like me, he had lived in the Greater China Region for many years and was very competent in Mandarin.

Meeting him was a real adrenalin rush, because it is rare even now that I encounter someone with a level of knowledge of Mandarin and everyday Chinese culture comparable to my own. This knowledge of Mandarin gave each of us a shared understanding of the other's experience with Chinese culture. We talked about how understanding Mandarin was one of the essential keys to comprehending Chinese culture. Our discussion revolved around the fact that Chinese people usually communicate indirectly, and how these different communication styles are imbedded, through the language, in Chinese people's behaviour. He then mentioned the importance of understanding the 36 Strategies and from that point, I knew I was about to embark on an incredible journey into knowledge that would expand the way I understood how Chinese people think, behave and negotiate.

He advised me that I should get to know the strategies intimately, because without this knowledge I would only float around the edges and never get to the core of Chinese cultural thinking.

Back in Australia I naively asked my staff, who were all Chinese, if they knew anything about the 36 Strategies. Not only did they all know the strategies, but several of them had their favourite strategies! Furthermore, they could easily tell me about situations they had been in when the strategies had been in play. Clearly this was something I needed to learn.

So I bought every book I could get my hands on about the 36 Strategies. However, I found them largely incomprehensible. Written in archaic language I could not find any linkages to contemporary business or daily life. The thought crossed my mind that I was heading down a dark road with no signposts.

It was clear to me that I had to find the connections between the 36 Strategies and contemporary business to truly understand, and therefore advise businesses about dealing with Chinese business people. The key to understanding Chinese culture is in knowing how the 36 Strategies are played out in everyday communication.

History of the 36 Strategies

The 36 Strategies originated from many centuries of inter-state conflict within China and are a collection of warfare wisdom that was not authored by one single person. The background to the 36 Strategies is that they have been attributed to Sun Tzu's, *The Art of War* (772 BCE to 481 BCE), or Zhuge Liang of the Three Kingdoms period (222 CE to 263 CE). Many business people, including myself, read texts about the 36 Strategies derived from *The Art of War* as we believe this excellent information is crucial to learning negotiation tactics from ancient Chinese wisdom. However, there was little written about how to connect the 36 Strategies with contemporary business culture. The 36 Strategies have been described as 'gems' that speak to the core of Chinese society, and are part of the 'collective unconscious' of most Chinese people.

During my years living in Taiwan I had no idea that the 36 Strategies even existed, therefore I had no comprehension of this collective unconscious. So deeply embedded in Chinese culture are the 36 Strategies that almost every Chinese person with whom I have ever discussed the strategies knows them, and knows them well. Love them or loathe them, the 36 Strategies are extremely well known to Chinese people, and almost completely unknown to Western people.

The 36 Strategies are used by Chinese people in all types of business dealings. They inform all areas of life, from children learning to haggle for food at the market, through to business people negotiating international deals. Yet we in the West know nothing about the 36 Strategies, and this is to our disadvantage when doing business within the Greater China Region.

When dealing with the Greater China Region, knowledge of the 36 Strategies is crucial. Without an understanding of how the 36 Strategies operate, Western business people can misinterpret situations, such as the purpose behind being invited out to eat by their Chinese contacts or that there are times when Chinese people say 'yes' when they really mean 'no'. Understanding the 36 Strategies means you can play the game of negotiation with your Chinese contacts. With no understanding it is similar to playing a sport when you do not know the rules – you are likely to come away second best.

You can use the 36 Strategies in all your dealings with Chinese people. The 36 Strategies will also help you in business in a Western context and with decisions in your personal life.

My passion is to share my research and knowledge of the 36 Strategies by providing practical contemporary examples so that my audiences have a clear understanding of how these strategies are used. Participants who attend my workshops and conference presentations are always amazed at how confident they feel once they understand this core piece of Chinese culture.

What Dao means

*Y*ou may be familiar with the word *Dao* written as *Tao*. Both *Dao* and *Tao* are Western attempts at the pronunciation of the Chinese character 道 using the Roman alphabet. The Chinese character 道 means 'way', 'path', 'route', or has even been described as meaning 'the key'.

The reason that you will see *Dao* also written as *Tao* is an accident of history. The first Westerners to develop a system to pronounce Chinese characters using the Roman alphabet were Thomas Wade and Herbert A. Giles who published a Chinese-English Dictionary in 1892. The Wade-Giles system shaped how people in the West learned to pronounce Mandarin. In 1958 the Wade-Giles system was entirely replaced in mainland China by the Hanyu Pinyin system, now known simply as Pinyin. While Pinyin is widely used across the Greater China Region, you will still see evidence of the Wade-Giles Romanisation in significant Chinese words. The naming of Beijing as Peking is an example of this. Beijing is in Pinyin. Peking is in Wade-Giles. The Western use of *Tao* is another example of the use of Wade-Giles, whereas *Dao* is in Pinyin.

I want this series of books on the 36 Strategies to be contemporary so I have called it *The Dao of Negotiation*. You can now easily work out that the translated title is 'the path of negotiation'. This book is your path to a method of negotiation that you can use when negotiating with Chinese people or negotiating in your everyday life.

How to pronounce Dao
The pronunciation of the 'ao' in *Dao* is similar to the sound you make when you pronounce the 'ow' in 'cow'.

Introduction to the Dao of Negotiation

*N*egotiating is hard and negotiating with Chinese people can be excruciatingly difficult.

When I discovered the real meaning and value of the 36 Strategies, I understood how much accumulated wisdom, knowledge, skill and experience business people from the Greater China Region bring to every business negotiation, and I want to share this with you.

I want you to be a great negotiator, and I know that you want to be a great negotiator too.

I learnt many years ago that Chinese people have a long history of being very good negotiators. Because of their long history they have a rich knowledge of the complexity of possibilities for different actions when they negotiate. The 36 Strategies gives them the rich vocabulary and structure to understand each negotiation in a way that helps them think about what they and their counterparts (the opposing side in a negotiation) are doing at any given moment.

The more you understand about each of the 36 Strategies the more skilful you will become in your negotiations. Additionally, greater knowledge of the 36 Strategies enables you to become better at recognising and then responding when the 36 Strategies are used on you. By reading this book, you will learn how to use them with your Chinese business counterparts, and also in your home country.

After many years living in Taiwan and in China, and working as a fluent Mandarin speaker, I have learnt that the 36 Strategies are essential keys to understanding Chinese business culture.

Where did you learn about negotiating?

Do you do much negotiating? We are not talking about simply striking a deal on the price, but really haggling over all the elements of the deal. You know you have achieved a successful negotiation when you reach a price low enough to satisfy the buyer and high enough to satisfy the seller.

In most Western countries we tend not to haggle for groceries or fruit and vegetables. Taxis always have meters. The goods in Western shops all tend to have fixed prices, and questions like, "*What will you do for cash?*" and "*Is that the best price you can offer?*" are considered displays of confidence in negotiating for a bargain.

Most Western business people do not grow up in cultures where they have to negotiate for the things they purchase. Generally the experience of negotiating for goods and services is only occasional. As a result most people's knowledge of, and skills in, negotiation tends to be relatively low, probably limited to purchasing a car or a house. If you only do something very occasionally you are unlikely to develop extensive knowledge in that activity. How often have you bought a house or a car? Even if you buy a new car every year and negotiate the price every time, this skill is still only used once a year, and because of this infrequency your negotiating skills are unlikely to be highly developed.

Therefore there is no endless practice, and there are no opportunities for learning the valuable lessons of negotiating on low value transactions. Mostly it will be large purchases you negotiate on.

From a language point of view, when you do not do something often, there is no need to talk about it. Consequently in the West we do not have much language for talking about negotiating. It is generally only in our adult life if we enrol in a business course that we might, just might, get some theory about how to negotiate, and perhaps a little practice in asking for what we want. Mostly that is the extent of your negotiation practice. This is why negotiation is hard. It is because we simply don't learn much about how to do it, have little language to discuss it, and few of us in Western countries get much practice at building our negotiation skills.

The Negotiation Challenge

So what happens when you meet a negotiator across a boardroom table who started learning the art and craft of negotiation as a child? Someone who has been haggling in street markets for food every day of their lives and is now a practiced negotiator who is part of a team with a shared language and history of negotiation?

- What usually happens is you lose and they win!
- The experienced negotiator gets the better price and you do not get what you want.
- Their team can use their shared language to assess what is going on in the negotiation so they can plan smart moves.

And it gets worse
- That shared language and history make it easy to understand and share strategic plans while you are left bewildered.
- You wonder what happened when you are exhausted and discover you just spent the evening talking intensely to someone who was not the best person to talk to about the final deal.
- On the night before you fly out of China you realise you still have not got the deal you were after and end up not clinching that important contract.

All of this leaves you with the absolute paralysing certainty that negotiating with Chinese business people is excruciating.

Books like *Getting to YES* are texts we might be introduced to in our twenties or even later, once our business role begins to require us to negotiate. We start as novices late in life.

If we are lucky we may begin to develop a simple language that we can employ when we negotiate. The language of Western business education is very genteel, and includes words like 'Negotiate', 'Cooperate', 'Compromise', 'Mediate', and 'Arbirtrate'. It may extend to 'Bargain' and 'Haggle".

There are no fundamental Western cultural stories that are particularly instructive about how to negotiate. There are very few role models. As a business person you will probably have read some case studies about the really big players and their massive negotiations. However, you need to be motivated in order to get to know the stories, the people and the negotiation strategies they used. This motivation to learn about negotiation generally happens at about the time you realise you need negotiation skills. Which is usually a little bit too late!

Not only that, but those big Western business stories offer no help for the daily game of strategic negotiation that is routinely played when you seek to do business with Chinese people. The big stories do not help you to understand why you cannot get to talk with the person you need to or what to do when they are running you ragged with banquets and sightseeing and other activities, leaving you feeling that there is nothing you can do to get them to the negotiating table!

It is unlikely your young children will grow up knowing the lessons from those business stories of negotiation. Only if they follow you into business might such knowledge be developed. This is completely different to the experience of Chinese people growing up in the Greater China Region.

Children growing up within the Greater China Region learn about the 36 Strategies, just as Western children learn sayings such as 'Don't cry over spilt milk', 'Don't count your chickens before they hatch', or 'A bird in the hand is worth two in the bush'. However, there are some very major differences in the nature of these sayings and stories.

The Western sayings are very focused around emotional control and expectation management, and do not have anything to do with negotiation or strategy. There is also no particular structure to the collection of sayings that a child in a Western country may learn.

The 36 Strategies are explicitly about negotiation, and there are an array of strategies that can be used to get what you want. The strategies are highly structured and inform action.

Negotiation is a skill that requires understanding and practice. Chinese people are often described as being shrewd in business and confident negotiators. Not only does Chinese culture encapsulate the practice of negotiation in the 36 Strategies, but negotiation is also a normal practice of their everyday life. A common Chinese saying is 'Everything is negotiable'. China is full of markets where people are always doing a deal. They may be simply negotiating the price of vegetables and other essential daily items, or something large like a business or property. Consequently, Chinese people learn to negotiate from a very young age.

This is so unlike most Western people's experience of negotiation, which is often limited to haggling in the market while on holidays, or negotiating at the boardroom table, with nothing in between.

Plan of the 36 Strategies and Introduction to Strategies 1 – 6

So far you know that there are 36 Strategies. You may well be wondering why has this book only got six strategies, and why these six? What about the other 30 strategies? What are they and when will I learn about them?

I am introducing you to the 36 Strategies, six strategies at a time for several reasons. As previously stated, my primary goal, which applies to all my work, is simple. I want you to be a great negotiator. The 36 Strategies will help you think differently about every negotiation you will ever be a part of .

I want every person who reads these books to be able to develop great skills, similar to Chinese business people, so you too can become a great negotiator.

The first reason I have presented only six strategies in this book *Tame the Tiger: Negotiating from a position of power,* is because within Chinese culture, the 36 Strategies are arranged and thought about in six groups of six strategies. Therefore it makes sense for me to introduce them to you in this authentic and grouped manner that will help you to both understand and use them effectively.

This book examines the **Advantageous Strategies**. These are the strategies to use when everything is going well for you in the negotiation and you decide you are in a superior position. You will discover more about the other groups of strategies in later books in *The Dao of Negotiation* series.

My second reason for including only six strategies at a time is that I want you to really get to know and to be able to use the strategies. In addition to having studied Mandarin myself, I have taught Mandarin and Chinese culture to hundreds of people over the past twenty years. I have learnt how to arrange very unfamiliar information in a way that helps people learn and, utilise what is being taught.

I know that if I introduce all 36 Strategies at once, even with the really useful and simple structure I have developed for *The Dao of Negotiation*, you are likely to be overwhelmed, and may confuse one strategy with another, and with that confusion, I will not be achieving our shared goal of you becoming a great negotiator. It will take time for you to really get to understand and to practice recognising and using each strategy.

Which brings us to my third reason. Because I want you to really get to know and to be able to see how you can use each of the 36 Strategies I will first introduce you to the original translation, before going on to explain what it all means and how to use it. If you have read *The Art of War* you might be familiar with these archaic Chinese stories. Each story illustrates a Strategy using an episode from Chinese history. The stories are told using the Chinese words for people and places. Unless you are familiar with Mandarin or Cantonese languages, you are likely to find these names challenging to recall and keep track of.

Don't worry – I do not want to scare you or overwhelm you. I use the Chinese names only in the introduction to each strategy. Then I translate each ancient story into contemporary English and illustrate the story with modern day examples of the strategy's use.

You do not have to spend any time on the Chinese names if you do not want to. However, if you want to build business connections with China or Chinese people, becoming familiar with Chinese names and their pronunciation will be time well spent. If you want to develop a friendship with someone, saying their name correctly goes a long way. To learn how to pronounce Mandarin Chinese correctly visit **www.pronouncemandarin.com**.

A key concept in developing business in the Greater China Region is 'Friends before business'. Why would you do business with people who are not your friends? So build the friendship as part of building the business relationship. Pronouncing people's names correctly is a small yet important step towards building a friendship. You will learn more about this important Chinese concept 'Friends before business' as you learn more about the 36 Strategies.

Greater China Region

You will notice that I mainly use the phrase 'Greater China Region'. You will also read elsewhere about the People's Republic of China, China and mainland China. They are phrases that have slightly different meanings and historical origins. According to Wikipedia:

China, or officially the People's Republic of China (PRC), is the world's second-largest state by land area. Governed by the Communist Party of China, it exercises jurisdiction over 22 provinces, five autonomous regions, four direct-controlled municipalities (Beijing, Tianjin, Shanghai and Chongqing) and the Special Administrative Regions of Hong Kong and Macau, and also claiming sovereignty over Taiwan.

The term mainland China was coined by the Kuomintang (KMT Party) after receiving control of Taiwan from Japan after World War II. By 1949, the KMT – led by the Republic of China (ROC) government – was defeated in the Chinese Civil War and fled to the island of Taiwan where the KMT pledged to retake the mainland. The KMT considers both sides of the Taiwan Strait (including Taiwan), as one nation, whereas Taiwan's Democratic Progressive Party (DPP) considers only mainland China as China, and Taiwan as a separate entity and country.

The Greater China Region refers to:

- China, or (more correctly) the People's Republic of China
- Taiwan
- Hong Kong
- Macau

While there are large Chinese communities in Malaysia and Singapore, they are not generally considered part of the Greater China Region.

Gender-Neutral Language

Please note that the original archaic Chinese stories were not composed in gender-neutral language, and I do want to remain consistent with the stories in my presentation of the 36 Strategies. However, gender-neutral language will be used in the rest of the discussions and examples.

How the 36 Strategies are grouped

For ease of use and learning the 36 Strategies will be grouped in six useful categories.

In each book I will introduce six strategies. For each strategy I will:

- Explain the original story.
- Provide examples of how the strategy is used against you.
- Give you strategies to counteract the strategies when used on you.
- Illustrate how you can use the strategy.
- Show ways you can use the strategy in a Western business environment.

In this book, *Tame the Tiger: Negotiating from a position of power*, we will be looking at Strategies 1 - 6, which are the **Advantageous Strategies**. These strategies are most useful when the strategist is in a position of power.

Advantageous
Strategies

Fool the emperor to cross the sea means to "*act in the open while hiding your real intentions*"

Moving about in the shadows, favouring isolated places or hiding behind screens will only attract suspicion. To lower an enemy's guard you must act in the open, hiding your true intentions under the guise of common everyday activities.

*I*n 643 CE, the Chinese emperor wanted to attack Korea, but he was not confident about sailing across the sea. The emperor's chief general led him down a dark tunnel to a big wooden room where they feasted for several days. Unbeknownst to the emperor, the room was on board the ship and, distracted by the party, he was unaware that he had been sailing across the sea.

In this scenario, the emperor was fooled by his top general, who '*acted in the open*' so that the emperor '*lowered his guard*' because the environment felt safe. The top general's '*true intentions were hidden under the guise*' of the party, and he managed to get the emperor to sail across the sea.

Strategy One - **Fool the emperor to cross the sea**, requires the strategist to '*act in the open and hide their true intentions*', and because of this openness people rarely realise Strategy One is being played out.

When going into an unfamiliar place, if you can 'look like you belong there', then you are far less likely to stand out and be unfavourably noticed.

In military situations where ordinary camouflage schemes are used, such as moving troops into dark secluded spaces, the troops can be easily detected because the other side becomes suspicious and will actively seek them out in potential hiding places.

If Strategy One is played out on you, then you are the emperor and the person fooling you is the person you are doing business with. Let's look at several ways that Strategy One may be used with Chinese people and also when negotiating with Western people in your home country.

Negotiating with Chinese People

EXAMPLE ONE
Strategy One in action (against you)

When you visit China you are likely to be picked up at the airport by your Chinese contact, and then taken out to a restaurant, which generally makes you feel more relaxed, so you lower your guard. The general thinking of a Western business person is that the real business will commence the following day, at the first formal meeting, and therefore there is no need to be on guard during the meal the night before. You are fed delicious food and probably given too much alcohol. The atmosphere is relaxed and not business-like at all, so you may feel it is safe to let your guard down, because they are *'acting in the open and hiding their real intentions'*.

Even though Chinese people are very hospitable and like to share their amazing array of wonderful food, when you are in this situation it is important to remember that there is another agenda being played out. The dinner is often used to find out crucial information from you, about you and your company, before you begin the formal meetings the following day. Alternatively, you are presented with a new issue that is likely to worry you and keep you awake the whole night. The next day you will be exhausted and not the sharp negotiator you might otherwise be. So your Chinese contacts now have the edge on you.

It is common for a Western business person to mis-interpret social situations when dealing with Chinese business people, because often English words used in a Chinese context can carry a different meaning. An example of this is when a Chinese person uses the word 'friend'. Chinese people often describe a person as their friend on the first meeting. In a Western context, a friend is a person you have known for a long time, but the idea of calling you a friend in a Chinese context is the signal to commence a business relationship.

We often hear that friendship is important to Chinese people, and we can be misled into believing all the socialising and entertaining that is conducted during business negotiations is for the development of this very important friendship. By fixating on developing the friendship with your Chinese counterpart, you may not see what is really going on within the wider business deal. This can result in saying "*yes*" to something that you should not have said yes to, or discussing the price of the product in question too early in the process. This can put you in an awkward position for the rest of the discussions. Sometimes there can be no coming back from this situation.

EXAMPLE ONE
Guarding yourself against Strategy One

Keep in mind that any time you are participating in business discussions with Chinese people you are entering a game where you will probably have some or even all of the 36 Strategies played out on you. An informal dinner may appear to be unimportant and unrelated to business, however it is all part of the deal. Often when you are invited into a familiar, friendly and safe place, you may forget that you are in a business situation.

It is important to be aware that even if you feel comfortable with your Chinese business counterparts, you need to remain alert and not let your guard down, regardless of the nature of the social activity. Business with Chinese people does not start the day after you land in the country. Business commences the minute you meet.

EXAMPLE TWO
Strategy One in action (against you)

A common method for Chinese people when using Strategy One is to ask what you would like to see in China. You may tell them that you want to see the Great Wall and the Forbidden City because these are world-famous structures that you have heard about and have always wanted to see. You then feel proud of yourself because you have taken control of the situation but, in reality, you have been led into setting up your own environment, where your Chinese contact is able to hide their true intentions while taking you on the tour of these famous sights. So even before the sightseeing commences this sense of control that you have been given is likely to make you feel comfortable, and it is easy to lower your guard.

In this scenario you have placed yourself in the open. When climbing the Great Wall your Chinese contact may ask you something regarding the forthcoming deal that was completely unexpected. In this situation you say 'yes' to something that in another situation you would have preferred to say 'no' to. This puts you into a corner that is difficult to get out of. The question to you may be something like, *"Can you deliver your product a month earlier than the original date?"* or *"Can you lower the price?"* In Strategy One, unexpected challenges are often carried out in the open so the recipient is unaware of the situation.

EXAMPLE TWO
Guarding yourself against Strategy One

Be aware that when you are asked what you would like to see in China, this is often a method of encouraging you to set up a situation where you feel comfortable or in charge, so that Strategy One can be used on you. Even when you are being taken sightseeing to places you want to see with your Chinese business counterparts, you should remember that you are really there to discuss business. Expect the unexpected.

Key Points when Strategy One is used against you

- When doing business with Chinese people, if you feel like you are in a safe place, it is probably a dangerous place.
- Business with Chinese people commences the minute you meet.
- A Chinese person may call you a 'friend' even though they have just met you. This often signals the commencement of a business relationship, as opposed to the Western social meaning of 'friend'.

How can you use Strategy One on your Chinese contacts, either when visiting them in the Greater China Region or when they visit you in your home country? Also, how can you use Strategy One when doing business within your own country?

I now wish to share two examples when negotiating with Western people where you can take charge of the negotiation by using Strategy One. In this way your business counterpart becomes the emperor whom you will fool.

EXAMPLE THREE
Enacting Strategy One

When you are entertaining a Chinese delegation, a way of applying Strategy One is to set up a familiar environment when you greet the Chinese group, by presenting them with their itinerary translated into Chinese characters. Even if your Chinese visitors are quite competent in English, they will feel more comfortable if their schedule is in their own language. Once you have presented your guests with their itinerary and gained their confidence, you can organise another familiar environment by taking them out for a meal. Chinese business people often feel relaxed when welcomed with the familiar scenario of eating with their business colleagues.

To use Strategy One when hosting the first meal, it is a good idea to choose a restaurant centred around eating as a group, as this is a familiar way of eating for Chinese people. A meal with many shared dishes of lovely food, and frequent *gumbei* (which translates as "dry glass"and means 'bottoms up'!) toasts by the host to acknowledge guests will soon have them feeling very comfortable. Then, during the meal, you could ask them a question that may be challenging, as they will now be relaxed and therefore will not expect you to ask anything out of the ordinary. By providing documents in Chinese and hosting a dinner as a group you can *act in the open, under the guise of common everyday activities*.

Negotiating in a Western Environment

**EXAMPLE FOUR
Enacting Strategy One**

You can use Strategy One when advertising a new product. Disguise your new product so it looks like something familiar, and therefore does not attract suspicious attention. Potential customers are unlikely to feel threatened in a familiar environment and therefore may consider buying your product. A good way of applying Strategy One is to advertise your product on a morning television segment, where many products are marketed as 'news'. Products advertised in this television segment often look like regular news. However, morning television is often more about advertising than news. In this way, it is difficult for potential customers to distinguish between the news and the advertising of a product. Advertising your product in this kind of format means that you are *hiding your true intentions under the guise of common everyday activities.*

Key Points when using Strategy One

- Use the familiar to introduce the unfamiliar.
- Learn about your counterpart or target so you know what makes them comfortable, and what makes them uncomfortable.
- Use translated materials to get your international business guests to feel secure.

Strategy Two

Besiege Wei to rescue Zhao *means "to look for and focus on their Achilles heel, which is their vulnerability"*

When the enemy is too strong to attack directly, then attack something he holds dear. Know that in all things he cannot be superior. Somewhere there is a gap in the armour, a weakness that can be attacked.

*I*n 354 BCE during the Warring States period in China, the small Kingdom of Zhao was attacked by the large powerful Kingdom of Wei. Wei's military force was huge compared to Zhao's army, so Zhao decided not to confront the Wei army on the battleground. Instead, Zhao's allies used Strategy Two - **Besiege Wei to rescue Zhao** to besiege the Wei capital, which had been left relatively unguarded. The Wei capital sent desperate messages back to the Wei troops saying that they needed urgent help, and the Kingdom of Zhao strategically allowed these messages to get through, so that the Wei troops would go back to the Wei capital to defend it. In the rush to get back to their capital the Wei army panicked and split off in all directions. As a result, the Wei troops did not operate as a group, and instead were separated into small individual units. In their weakened state, Zhao's allies were easily able to attack them on the open road as they tried to get back to the Wei capital.

In this story, the Wei Kingdom was the attacking enemy, or opponent, with a very powerful army that was *'too strong to attack directly'*. Using its allies, the Zhao Kingdom strategically placed the Wei troops in a position where they no longer had a unified front and were therefore weakened. The Zhao Kingdom found *'a gap in the armour'* of the Wei troops, and through this gap in the armour they attacked the Wei army. The Wei troop's weakness was that they thought the only resource required to win a battle was a large army. What they did not realise was that just having a large army was not enough. They also needed a clever army who were able to look at situations from many different angles.

When Strategy Two is used on you, your Chinese contact will strategically focus on your weakness, so they can find the *'gap in your armour'*. Strategy Two is often used on individuals employed within large companies that are too strong to confront directly. Confrontation is conducted through focusing on something the target *'holds dear'* – their weakest point – to reach a desired outcome.

Negotiating with Chinese People

EXAMPLE ONE
Strategy Two in action (against you)

When you travel to the Greater China Region to meet with business people, they will commonly have a larger group of people as part of their negotiating team than you will have in your team. Chinese culture generally operates as a group, or collective culture. As a result, Chinese people are usually more comfortable being part of large groups. In this group culture a Chinese negotiating team is likely to be comprised of several people.

Western culture is a lot more individualistic. Westerners are more likely to feel comfortable travelling alone or in small groups. This individualism extends into the organisation and operation of Western business. If you are meeting with Chinese people to do business, you will probably be outnumbered by your Chinese counterparts.

It is also likely that the Chinese business people you are dealing with will have done a lot of research on you and your company. This means your hosts will know a lot about you. The more they know about you, the better chance they will have of locating your weaknesses and therefore finding a *gap in your armour*.

One way Chinese people use Strategy Two is by splitting your group up, so your team members are separated from each other. You and your colleagues each become one person amongst several Chinese people. You will then be challenged or asked lots of questions beyond your area of expertise. For example, you may find you are asked questions about pricing, when your expertise is in marketing, while the person in your group with expertise in pricing will be strategically ignored by your Chinese counterparts. This strategy is used to create tension. When you are asked unexpected questions, you are likely to get nervous because of your lack of expertise, and give an answer that puts your company in a difficult position, causing yet more tension in your team.

Questions might be asked when your group is together but spread out, in situations such as walking as a group to the next destination. The individuals in your team can get separated as you walk to the next destination, which means they become isolated from each other, and thus becoming vulnerable to challenging questions.

Alternatively, the most vulnerable person in your group may get isolated by being put into a different car to be taken to the next destination, where they are surrounded by the Chinese group and asked questions that are not in their field of expertise.

EXAMPLE ONE
Guarding yourself against Strategy Two

Operating in a small group, in comparison to the larger Chinese group, will make you more vulnerable. To guard against Strategy Two, you will need to ensure the person or people in your group lacking expertise in key areas are always with other members of your group, no matter what your Chinese hosts do to separate your team from one another. In this way you always present a unified front.

Sometimes it is not possible for you to travel with the other members of your group, so it is crucial you are on guard, because the Chinese group will be looking for 'a gap in your armour'. As a result, Strategy Two may be played out on you when you least expect it. Therefore you need to organise several responses to guard against Strategy Two.

One approach is for your team to prepare in advance for the possibility of getting separated from each other and being 'grilled' over challenging topics, by developing and rehearsing a consistent standard response to all challenging questions. Something like *"that is an interesting question. I am keen to share this with my team and then we can get back to you"*. Note I suggest saying 'we' will respond, so there is no expectation that the vulnerable individual will do the responding. This way, even if your team members do get separated from each other and the most vulnerable member of your team is asked a difficult question, they will have a well-rehearsed neutral 'push back' in reply. This will keep the relationship with your Chinese counterparts intact, and the negotiation on track.

EXAMPLE TWO
Strategy Two in action (against you)

We all have our strengths and weaknesses. When Strategy Two is in play, the focus is on your weaknesses, in order to find the *'gap in your armour'*. When our weaknesses or preferences are focused on, we often show our vulnerabilities.

For example, if you are passionate about a topic such as the environment, you may be inclined to get upset about the air quality and other environmental issues in China. In their research about you, your Chinese counterparts are likely to have learned about this interest of yours. Through use of Strategy Two they can turn your interest into a vulnerability.

You may be provoked to comment on the environment in China, and possibly become emotional, which may lead to criticism of your hosts or of China itself. Such expression of your passions or convictions can become a distraction from the real issue of the business. While you are distracted, it is easier for your Chinese business counterparts to gain the upper hand in the negotiation. In a group setting, you might also consult other members of your group in an anxious, angry or upset state, which may result in the whole group becoming distracted and effectively weakened.

EXAMPLE TWO
Guarding yourself against Strategy Two

The more you know about yourself and your own responses, and the greater control you have over them, the less likely it is that Strategy Two can be played out on you in this way. It is as crucial in successful negotiations, as it is in much of life, that you understand your vulnerabilities and strongly held beliefs. Without full awareness of your passions, no matter how important they are to you, those passions can also be your weaknesses. To protect yourself against your passions becoming a vulnerability when conducting business with Chinese people, it is useful to keep your opinions to yourself and refrain from commenting.

This injunction to keep your strongly held opinions to yourself is particularly relevant when visiting mainland China or working with people from China. One of the most significant aspects of Western culture is its many freedoms. As a Western business person you are likely to come from a country where free speech is respected, expected and encouraged, and possibly even protected by law.

Do consider that China has different legal and cultural attitudes to freedom of speech. Western business people need to consider that disclosing such privately held views may be inappropriate. Getting upset about such issues will be counterproductive if your aim is to finalise a business deal. Focusing on your differences merely consumes valuable energy that you will require for the negotiation.

Key Points when Strategy Two is used against you

- In preparation for your meeting expect that your Chinese counterparts will have conducted considerable research on your company.
- Operate as a group by presenting a unified front, to guard against your Chinese contacts focusing on your individual vulnerabilities.
- Be aware of your passions and avoid becoming provoked on an issue you are passionate about which is not connected to the business at hand.

EXAMPLE THREE
Enacting Strategy Two

As well as being a group culture, Chinese culture is also hierarchical. This means that there are strong social structures giving people within the culture a place relative to everyone else. This hierarchical aspect of the culture is very strong and every member in a family is named in such a way as to let everyone know where they fit into the hierarchy. So everyone will know who the 'eldest sister' is by how she is addressed, and that she is older is because she sits higher up in the hierarchy compared to the 'youngest sister'. Every aunt and uncle will be similarly named and numbered.

What this means in a negotiation with a Chinese company is that their negotiating team will be structured in a strongly hierarchical manner. Your task is to work out who is the leader and who is working under the leader, and what is the correct order of the hierarchy. This is important information that needs to be determined and understood by everyone in your negotiating team. Sorting out the hierarchy will take time. It will be well worth the effort to research as much as you can about your Chinese contacts and their power relationships with each other.

Do not just automatically think that because your main Chinese contacts studied abroad they will want to do business in a Western manner. Many Chinese business people have studied business aboard, and they will therefore understand how Western culture and Western business culture operates. However, you will find that most Chinese people will conduct business in the Chinese way. This will include, especially from China, valuing their hierarchy. Additionally, it is more likely that the younger team members will have Western education experiences. It is worth remembering that because they are younger and are likely to be lower in the hierarchy, and therefore have the least power. The style of negotiation will be controlled by the senior members of the Chinese team.

As well as working with the power hierarchy of the opposing negotiating team, Strategy Two is about knowing the strengths and weaknesses of the person with whom you are dealing. Your main contact is highly unlikely to be the decision maker whose approval is required to clinch your deal. If you are travelling to China you may have no contact with this important person until you are ready to close the deal. A Chinese company is likely to use a Western-educated Chinese person to help you feel at ease, however, this person will not be running the negotiations.

A useful way to research your Chinese contacts is by locating representatives from overseas government trade or business departments or international Chambers of Commerce operating in China, as they are likely to be able to easily access information about your contacts. Understanding if your contacts are currently connected with the Chinese government can be very useful, because they are likely to connect you with the correct government decision-makers.

Your contacts may already have experience conducting deals with overseas companies. You can enquire as to why they are interested in dealing with your company. This style of curiosity will demonstrate that you are not afraid and are prepared to ask questions that are slightly confrontational.

Playing the 'divide the team' game yourself by separating the Chinese group, so that there is one Chinese person surrounded by several members of your team, will present strength and give you the opportunity to ask challenging questions to an individual Chinese person.

Negotiating in a Western Environment

EXAMPLE FOUR
Enacting Strategy Two

Strategy Two can be used where you advertise a product to appeal to adults by using children in the advertising campaign. A car company may focus on the safety of children while travelling in the car. This could be achieved by emphasising particular features that will keep the child safe. By using children, the car company focuses on what parents *'hold dear'*, which is their children, and thus the car company is able to find *'a gap in the armour'* of parents. In turn, the parents become interested in buying the vehicle, with their main concern being the safety of their children.

Key Points when using Strategy Two

- Learn all you can about your opponent.
- Aim to never go to a negotiation alone.
- Understand your clients' or counterparts' vulnerabilities.

Strategy Three

Murder with a borrowed knife means "to conserve energy by using another person's strength"

When the enemy's intention is obvious and the ally's attitude hesitant, induce the ally to fight the enemy while preserving one's own strength.

*D*uring the Warring States Period in China between 475 and 221 BCE, Fei Wuji was the vice-premier of the Kingdom of Chu. He was secretly jealous of the warrior Xi Wan who was favoured highly by the premier, Nang Wa. Fei Wuji's jealousy drove him to the point that he wanted to kill Xi Wan, but he was unable to perform this murder himself because he knew it would destroy his reputation. Premier Nang Wa planned to visit Xi Wan, and Xi Wan was so excited he asked Fei Wuji what he should do to impress the premier. Fei Wuji applied Strategy Three - **Murder with a borrowed knife** by suggesting to Xi Wan that, because his sword was famous throughout the land, he should present it to Premier Nang Wa.

Thinking that this was a good idea he quickly positioned his soldiers, dressed in full armour, down both sides of his reception area. He laid his polished sword before him to await Premier Nang Wa's visit. Meanwhile, Fei Wuji warned Premier Nang Wa that he had heard a rumour that Xi Wan wanted to assassinate him. Premier Nang Wa brushed off the rumour and rode off to visit Xi Wan. When Premier Nang Wa saw Xi Wan's troops in full combat gear waiting on each side of Xi Wan, with the polished sword drawn before him, Premier Nang Wa thought it was a trap, and ordered his troops to attack Xi Wan. However his troops did not kill Xi Wan. Devastated at the thought that Premier Nang Wa believed this rumour, Xi Wan committed suicide. After that incident Premier Nang Wa only listened to Fei Wuji, because he believed Fei Wuji had saved his life, and as a result Fei Wuji became extremely powerful.

In this story Xi Wan was driven to suicide, because he could not live with the knowledge that Premier Nang Wa had believed he would have wanted to assassinate him. Xi Wan was placed in a positon where suicide for him became his only option. In the creation of this scenario, Fei Wuji strategically 'murdered Xi Wan with a borrowed knife', and Premier Nang Wa respected Fei Wuji's advice, as he believed that Fei Wuji had saved his life.

When dealing with Chinese people and Strategy Three is used on you, it will be by a Chinese person of lower authority who will ask you difficult questions or will have the difficult issues directed to them, because the leader is 'preserving their strength'.

Negotiating with Chinese People

EXAMPLE ONE
Strategy Three in action (against you)

When you are meeting with your Chinese contacts, it will not be the most important person in the Chinese negotiating team who asks the difficult questions such as "*can you lower the price*?" It will be a person of the lower status who will ask these questions. Likewise, your senior Chinese contact will not criticise your proposals, as complaints will be done by the person with a lower status, in order to conserve the leader's strength and reputation. Strategy Three enables the leader to '*preserve their strength*', while other issues are still being worked out.

A way of understanding how Strategy Three works is to imagine you are in a chess match. The king is the most important piece on the chessboard. Victory comes when you can place your opponent's king in checkmate. Yet of all the chess pieces it is the king that moves the least. To locate the most powerful person in a Chinese group, look for the person who says the least and has minimal interaction with the opposing side, just like the king on the chessboard.

EXAMPLE ONE
Guarding yourself against Strategy Three

Introduce your group to the Chinese group in such a way as to demonstrate a clear hierarchy. Now this may not be how you normally operate because Western business practices generally reflect the flat business structures and short power distances common in Western cultures. A Western negotiating team is likely to be composed of people who hold a similar level of authority.

Power distance refers to the way in which **power** is distributed, and the extent to which the less powerful accept that **power** is distributed unequally. People in some cultures accept a higher degree of inequality in the distribution of **power** than people in other cultures.

Structuring your negotiating team in a hierarchical manner for the purpose of achieving your goals with your Chinese counterparts will give the Chinese group the opportunity to expose the hierarchical structure of their group. By matching their structure you will make this disclosure easier, and you will be more certain of the relative status of each member of their group.

The other benefit of using a hierarchical structure, where everyone has a specific task or role, is that it will save your team a lot of energy when negotiating with Chinese people. Negotiating through a different organisational structure to your Chinese counterparts, particularly when in their country, will be exhausting, and may not be understood by them. If you operate in an egalitarian environment where all of your team participate relatively equally, it is likely you will all, including the leader of your team, exhaust yourselves. In the Chinese negotiating team only the people below the leader will have obviously worked hard. Meanwhile, the leader of the Chinese team will have conserved their energy. This will make it much easier for them to get what they want, and for you to go home empty handed!

EXAMPLE TWO
Strategy Three in action (against you)

When you are communicating with Chinese manufacturers, you are likely to find Strategy Three being used on you. Many Western companies have products or components manufactured in China. For this to work successfully, Western business people need to communicate with factories. When difficulties arise, as they often do, the Westerner wants to talk with the Chinese manager or owner. When there is a problem, getting hold of this person becomes incredibly difficult, and can sometimes feel impossible. No matter how hard you try, you can never get this key contact to answer your emails or to get them on the phone.

So then you decide you need to visit the factory, in order to see your contact face-to-face. You or your staff believe you have negotiated your visit to include a face-to-face meeting with your elusive Chinese counterpart. However, when you arrive in China, you are told they are too busy to see you. You end up settling for second (or third) best, and are expected to deal with someone a few rungs below the head person, because this main decision-maker is *preserving their energy*.

Example Two
Guarding yourself against Strategy Three

In the Western business environment, when a person you are accustomed to dealing with leaves your supplier, while you might miss them at a personal level, their replacement is usually trained in such a way that the two of you are able to continue working together fairly seamlessly. The 'relationship' is really between your companies, and each of you are representatives of your companies, so things continue as usual. There is no need to have several contacts just in case your counterpart leaves.

However, when working with a Chinese company, you need to develop multiple relationships. As you are almost certainly going to be dealing with someone below the head person, therefore you need to develop relationships in the factory with more than one person. This is particularly important, because if the person you have been communicating with leaves the factory you may no longer have a reliable contact who understands your requirements. It is therefore crucial that you develop your relationship with at least two people who can answer your questions and follow up on any issues that arise.

Keep in mind that middle management in China is similar to their Western counterparts, in that they can be quite mobile and move from job to job. The important thing is to build up multiple contacts of similar status, and access the decision-maker within the same business, as you do not want to be left in the vulnerable position of no longer having a contact who knows you and is able to take your concerns to the senior management or business owner.

Key Points when Strategy Three is used against you

- Understand the hierarchy of the Chinese group so you know who the leader is.
- The leader is similar to the king on the chessboard, even though they move the least they are the most powerful member of the team.
- Develop relationships with at least two people who can help you address your issues in the Chinese company with whom you are dealing.

EXAMPLE THREE
Enacting Strategy Three

To use Strategy Three when you are dealing with Chinese people, the most crucial element is having a hierarchy that is clear to all members of your team. This hierarchical structure will give you the opportunity to have questions directed to a person of lower status than the leader, which means your leader gets to preserve their strength, just like the Chinese team leader. You need to decide on this hierarchy before you meet with your Chinese contacts. Remember your team is unlikely to be familiar with such a hierarchical way of working, as most Western businesses operate with much flatter structures, with little distance or difference in power between the top and lower levels. Working out the hierarchy in advance will help your team to understand what is expected of them.

You establish this hierarchy by introducing your team in order, from the most important to the least important person. You can also reinforce this hierarchy with seating, where the most important person sits in the middle and the next most important person sits on either side of them and so on, with the least important person at the end of the table.

Negotiating in a Western Environment

EXAMPLE FOUR
Enacting Strategy Three

You can use Strategy Three in a Western context through a pre-arranged delegation of tasks in the negotiation process, just as you would when negotiating a deal with a Chinese business. The people in your team to whom you delegate tasks need to be prepared so they can answer an array of questions from the opposite negotiating team. This will *conserve your energy and strength*. As a leader, you will need to be consistently clear with your team about your leadership model, which means knowing your team well enough to delegate tasks with confidence. Your staff need to be fully prepared, so they will feel confident about managing the questions and other issues that may arise. They need to know that conserving the leader's energy is part of the negotiating plan, so they will not come running to you with questions in front of your negotiating opponents.

Key Points when using Strategy Three

- Ensure your team is clear about their position within the unfamiliar hierarchy.
- The way you introduce your team, and where you all sit, will help reinforce the hierarchy you create for your team.
- Train your team in how to play this game, so you can conserve your energy and enable your company to do well in the negotiation.

Wait leisurely for an exhausted enemy
means "to exercise patience and wear them down"

It is advantageous to choose the time and place for battle. In this way you know when and where the battle will take place, while your enemy does not. Encourage your enemy to expend his energy in futile quests while you conserve your strength. When he is exhausted and confused, you attack with energy and purpose.

*I*n 684 BCE, the Qi army attacked the state of Lu, and the leader of Lu – Lu Zhuang Gong – decided to retaliate. Lu Zhuang Gong chose Chang Shao as the location for the battle. Cao Gui, who was a famous warrior, advised Lu Zhuang Gong on how to '*exhaust*' the Qi army, while the Lu army '*conserved their strength*'.

The Qi army launched the first round of attacks. Cao Gui, who was an expert strategist applied Strategy Four - **Wait leisurely for an exhausted enemy,** he persuaded Lu Zhuang Gong to react slowly while keeping up their defences at all times. Cao Gui did not want Lu Zhuang Gong to rush into the battle. The Qi army began to launch the second round of attacks, and they beat large drums to display their power. As instructed by Cao Gui, Lu Zhuang Gong continued to stay on the defensive and did not attempt to strike.

As a result, the Qi army thought the Lu army was timid and they continued to beat their drums, and attacked for the third time. After the third attack the Qi army had used a lot of energy, and were exhausted and confused. All the while, the Lu soldiers had been resting, and unlike the Qi army they were not exhausted. Consequently, when the battle began, the Lu soldiers quickly won, because the Qi army had little energy left to fight.

In this scenario Lu Zhuang Gong '*chose the time and place for battle*'. He therefore knew '*where the battle was going to take place*', and because the Lu army initially defended and did not fight, the Qi army thought the Lu army were timid. In reality, the Lu army encouraged the Qi army to '*expend their energy, while they conserved their strength*', and this drove the Qi army into a state of '*exhaustion and confusion*'. The Lu army were then able to attack '*with energy and purpose*'.

When Strategy Four is applied, your Chinese contact will try to put you in a position where they can easily '*exhaust you*'. Most negotiations with Chinese people are done in their own country. This means you are a visitor and therefore often in very unfamiliar surroundings. The purpose of this strategy is to create a situation where you become tired, which means you will probably run out of mental energy and be more likely to give your Chinese contact the price they want.

Negotiating with Chinese People

EXAMPLE ONE
Strategy Four in action (against you)

Strategy Four is very likely to be used on you when you visit China to conduct a negotiation. A likely scenario is where your Chinese contact picks you up from the airport and on the way to your hotel asks when you are flying out of China. The Western method of business communication is to be precise, and this often means that your natural response is to tell your contact the day and time of your departure. By giving them this information you have enabled your Chinese contact to determine the precise *'time for battle'*, which will be just when you are due to leave. You can guarantee that the night before you leave China there will be a late night and probably too much alcohol, leaving you exhausted for the meetings the next day.

In this scenario your contact has encouraged you to expend your energy, while they conserve their strength. When Strategy Four is being applied, you will be entertained and kept awake very late the night before your leave China. When socialising, Chinese people will often, in the course of one evening, go to a bar, then a restaurant and then to another bar. This will involve lots of getting in and out of cars, going in and out of hotels and restaurants, having more food than you really want to eat, and lots and lots of opportunities for *gumbei* to toast each and every one of your hosts, to the beauty of China, to your home country, and so on and so forth.

In such a scenario, Western business people often get to the point where they feel it is easier just to give the Chinese side the price they want, because the Westerners become mentally and sometimes physically exhausted. Additionally, because the time and place of negotiation is not within their control, and the departure time is fast approaching. Many Western business people feel they cannot return home and say to their colleagues "*I just couldn't get them to the negotiating table*". Consequently they can find themselves overwhelmed or in a state of panic near the end of their trip, and therefore end up accepting a lower price, or higher demands.

EXAMPLE ONE
Guarding yourself against Strategy Four

When you arrive in China to conduct a negotiation, your Chinese counterparts will definitely ask you about your departure time. Even though you will almost certainly have a return ticket with a fixed departure day and time, be vague in your reply to this seemly innocuous question. Strategy Four is a classic Chinese negotiation strategy.

The most effective way to respond to this probe for crucial information is to be imprecise when asked about your departure day and time.

The best response would be to indicate that you have yet to confirm your departure date and time. Persist with this as your response, and the Chinese hosts will understand that you will not tell them when you are leaving. It will not be regarded as rude to not answer absolutely truthfully. It will be seen as part of the way the game of negotiation is played!

Take your time answering these sorts of probing questions, and put some thought into thinking about the strategy that is likely to lay behind the question. It is not necessary for you to answer with complete accuracy. On these occasions imprecision is the correct response.

Example Two
Strategy Four in action (against you)

When Western business people visit China they generally spend about a week in the country. For many business people this is about as long as they feel they can be away from their workplace.

Whether you are on your first trip to China and are being introduced to your Chinese contact for the first time or you are an old hand and have made many trips to China, your Chinese contacts will seek to entertain you and monopolise your time so you *expend your energy*. As a result, many Western business people find they have little or no time to themselves. This means that every waking hour is filled with meetings, eating, drinking and sightseeing.

In this way, your Chinese contacts have control over all the locations you visit throughout your trip, often leaving you unaware of where you are being taken. This is likely to leave you in a vulnerable situation, because not only are you in a foreign country, but you are also taken out to many unfamiliar places. In this 'exhausted' state, when negotiating with your Chinese contacts, you are likely to come out on the worst end of a deal because you are always behind the game, whereas the Chinese people you are dealing with can remain calm and conserve their energy, because they are on their own territory and can control the time of the negotiation.

The other challenge this monopolisation of your time presents to Western business people is that it becomes difficult to meet other Chinese business people. It can also cut you off from other Western business people working in China whose experience you might be able to use to give you useful local intelligence. By having your time consumed you become unable to learn more about what is going on. In this way, your decision-making is controlled.

Example Two
Guarding yourself against Strategy Four

To protect yourself against being mentally and physically exhausted, you need to keep control of your time and the location of meetings. You can do this in several ways.

It is usual in China for business people to have their own personal driver, rather than using taxis, which can be hard to find, and even harder to direct, as almost no taxi driver will speak English or any other Western language! So organise with your hotel for a driver to meet you at the airport.

There are several advantages in getting your own driver from the airport to your hotel. It will elevate your status among your Chinese counterparts and suggest you understand something about how business is conducted in China. It will also get you to your hotel without having to negotiate the taxi fare AND fend off probing enquiries from your Chinese contacts before you have recovered from your flight. You are not relying on your Chinese counterparts to pick you up at the airport and you can keep your arrival and departure information private. You can also set the date and time for your first meeting.

This also allows you to make appointments with more than one company. Without giving yourself this degree of autonomy, you will find that the company that picks you up at the airport will control all your time, and prevent you seeing other businesses.

Other ways you can take charge include suggesting places to meet or inviting the Chinese team to a restaurant. As you may not know of many eating places in China, you can always invite them to your hotel for a meal, and this will give you control. If you are in a situation where it is not possible to exercise control over your itinerary, it is crucial that you keep as calm and relaxed as possible at all times, as this busy schedule is purposefully put in place to exhaust and confuse you.

Copy the example of the Chinese, who are excellent at closing their eyes whenever they are travelling somewhere. Even if they are not actually asleep, you will observe your Chinese counterparts taking every opportunity to rest. This is particularly true of the people with more status in the hierarchy, who, using Strategy Three - **Murder with a**

borrowed knife, leave others of lesser status to attend to the more mundane activities like making sure the driver has the correct address or checking that the restaurant table is booked, while the leader gets to conserve and restore their energy.

Should you decide you are exhausted and need some time away from the hustle and bustle of the program your Chinese hosts have arranged for you, you could say you need to call your family and spend some considerable time talking to them as you are far away from home. You will find your Chinese counterparts will respect this, as family always comes first within Chinese culture.

Key Points when Strategy Four is used against you

- It is a good idea to be imprecise when providing information such as the date and time you are leaving China. For example, "*I haven't confirmed my flight details yet*" regardless of whether it is true or not.
- When being taken to unfamiliar places to meet and eat, stay calm and do not let the situation exhaust you.
- When the situation allows, take some control by getting your own driver from the airport, and offering to host a meal at your hotel.

EXAMPLE THREE
Enacting Strategy Four

You can use Strategy Four on your Chinese contacts when hosting them on a visit to your country. This can be applied by designing their schedule so they have little time to themselves when in your country. When applying this strategy, you fill their time with meetings, sightseeing, shopping and dinners, and by using this busy schedule you can wait leisurely to exhaust them. A busy schedule leaves no time in your Chinese guests' schedule to have private discussions with their Chinese colleagues, and therefore limits the time available to them to prepare for the next meeting so they *'expend their energy'*.

Often when a Chinese person visits your country and you ask them when they are flying back to China, they do not provide a clear answer. They will probably say they have not yet confirmed their flight. However, in reality, they will know their departure details, as the Chinese government has tight controls on its citizens' travel schedules. Your guests will know this information before they leave. This imprecise style of communication is to prevent Strategy Four being played out on them.

Negotiating in a Western Environment

EXAMPLE FOUR
Enacting Strategy Four

Strategy Four can be used if you are engaged in a difficult negotiation and you have been instructed to come out with the best offer in a short space of time. To apply Strategy Four, you need to put something on the table at the meeting that is possibly only a distraction and definitely a surprise to the opposing group. Your counterparts are likely to become slightly anxious or confused while you remain very calm and cool-headed. By the time the negotiation eventually takes place the people with whom you are negotiating will be 'exhausted and confused', as they will have spent time and energy considering this new proposal or information you have injected into the negotiation, while you can relax and wait for them to make their next move in their 'exhausted' state.

This element of surprise is disorientating, and forces your counterparts to expend their time and energy discussing your unexpected new proposal, giving you the advantage.

Key Points when using Strategy Four

- Ensure your Chinese visitors have a full schedule of activities to limit their ability to talk together or to rest.
- Ensure you have one or two challenging ideas to throw onto the table to help destabilise your opponents.
- Be careful that you do not get caught up in any attempt to destabilise your own negotiating team.

Loot a burning house means "when there is a crisis there is an opportunity"

When the enemy suffers from a major crisis, seize the chance to gain advantage.

*D*uring the Three Kingdoms Period from 220 CE to 300 CE, there was a stand-off between Cao Cao and his enemies, Sun Quan and Zhou Yu, concerning the ownership of territories. In this battle Cao Cao had his ships burned, after he was tricked into chaining them together. As he had no ships left, and therefore no resources, he lost the battle against Sun Quan and Zhou Yu. Cao Cao decided to flee, leaving the territory he had controlled, in a state of chaos.

A third rival, Liu Bei, and his master strategist Zhuge Liang then invaded the territory that Cao Cao had left. Even though Sun Quan and Zhou Yu had won the territory, it was still in a state of considerable turmoil. This level of chaos provided an opportunity for an easy invasion for Liu Bei and Zhuge Liang. They did this by applying Strategy Five - **Loot a burning house**. Sun Quan and Zhou Yu did not realise they were being invaded. They were so focused on bringing order to the territory, they did not notice the new invaders. The battle that defeated Cao Cao had left destruction, and there were many valuables scattered about the countryside, which Liu Bei and his master strategist Zhuge Liang quickly collected. Sun Quan and Zhou Yu were more focused on restoring order and establishing control, and so they had failed to protect the riches. The chaos concealed Liu Bei and Zhuge Liang's actions, allowing them to help themselves to all the valuable items. They *seized the chance to take advantage*.

Strategy Five is used in situations where there has been a '*major crisis*', which creates opportunities for the strategist to '*take advantage*' of the disruption.

Negotiating with Chinese People

EXAMPLE ONE
Strategy Five in action (against you)

During and following the Global Financial Crisis of 2008 and 2009, many countries suffered serious debt. Combined with this debt crisis there was political instability, placing many countries in a vulnerable position. A large number of Chinese investment companies saw this global crisis as an opportunity to buy cheap properties and businesses overseas. These Chinese companies *seized the chance to gain advantage*. The desire for countries to reduce their debt level has provided many Chinese developers with the opportunity to purchase properties and businesses in other countries extremely cheaply. On many occasions China's available cash has offered other countries a way out of the financial chaos. It is not uncommon for people in financially and politically vulnerable positions to sell their assets for a lower price than they are actually worth.

EXAMPLE ONE
Guarding yourself against Strategy Five

Often in a crisis situation we are focused on the crisis as opposed to how to deal with it. Our judgement can become clouded by the turmoil and panic of the crisis, which generally places us in a position of trying to achieve the quickest way out of the difficult situation. By not thinking through the turmoil we are in, and looking at all options, we may not see that Strategy Five is being used on us, because our focus is on the turmoil. If we have financial difficulties, it is common to take the price that is offered as a way of getting out of these difficulties. In situations such as needing to sell properties or businesses to recoup money, we need to assess all options before making any quick decisions. Chinese business people are generally opportunistic and by using Strategy Five they are able to use a crisis to their advantage. Prior to making any financial decisions to get yourself out of a crisis, it is important to research all available options that may solve your financial problem.

Seek to always ensure you have access to resources or supporters, so that you can act quickly when you are aware of significant social or economic changes or when others' experience major reversals of fortune.

EXAMPLE TWO
Strategy Five in action (against you)

In 2010 Google left China following a dispute between the company and the Chinese government. The Chinese search engine, Baidu, contacted every Google corporate client in China and tried to win them over, since Google was no longer in operation in China. The dispute between Google and the Chinese government resulted in a crisis for Google, and their global reputation was at stake. During this major crisis, Baidu applied Strategy Five and seized the *'chance to gain advantage'*, because Google was consumed by their dispute with the Chinese government and were focused on upholding their global reputation.

EXAMPLE TWO
Guarding yourself against Strategy Five

Strategy Five may be used on you if you have a dispute with another company, and the strategist, usually a third party, uses this dispute to gain business for themselves. In this scenario you need to keep the information regarding the dispute to yourself, as this may be used to win business, in the same way that Baidu used Google's crisis.

For Google to have protected themselves against Strategy Five, in terms of damage to their reputation and in terms of enabling Baidu to take over their clients, it would have been beneficial for Google to have studied Chinese negotiation tactics in order to have a better understanding of what strategies may be used on them. Google approached the deal using a direct Western method. Essentially, it was Google's way or no way.

Now you may not agree with all aspects of the decision making processes of the Government of the People's Republic of China. However, when wanting to do business in a country it is important to understand and respect the local cultural nuances and requirements.

By treating China as they would any other country, Google managed to close off all avenues for any future re-entry into China, as they were not willing to compromise on what the Chinese government proposed. Even if they did not want to operate in China in the way the Chinese Government instructed, it would have been more beneficial for Google to resolve the situation without the relationship becoming irreparably damaged. The fact that this did not happen resulted in Google's business in China being consumed by a major local player who used Strategy Five to grow their own business. Additionally, Google's reputation in China has been damaged significantly.

Key Points when Strategy Five is used against you

- When faced with a crisis situation, focus on different ways of dealing with the situation, rather than on the crisis itself.
- Often what is the easy solution may not be the best solution.
- A crisis is likely to place you in a vulnerable position.

EXAMPLE THREE
Enacting Strategy Five

The 2008 milk formula scandal in China caused many Chinese consumers to lose confidence in domestic milk products. During this crisis several foreign companies who manufactured milk products began to export their milk formula to China. As Chinese parents panicked about the possible dangers of consumption of the domestic milk formula, this scandal provided an excellent opportunity for these foreign companies to substantially raise their prices.

To use Strategy Five, you need to keep current with social and political developments, and even weather conditions, going on in China, as situations may arise where you are able to *'seize an opportunity'* as soon as it presents itself. If you do not keep up with what is going in China, good opportunities may pass you by.

Foreign companies with good local intelligence are able to *'seize the opportunities'* and prosper from doing business with China when there is a product or service that is in demand and there is a shortage of that product or service due to a crisis.

Even if your product is in high demand, research is required as to how to market your product in China. You may also have to modify your product slightly, in order for it to be accepted in the Chinese market. In the case of milk formula, companies needed to redesign the packaging so that Chinese consumers were able to understand what they were buying, even though everything else about the product remained the same.

Negotiating in a Western Environment

EXAMPLE FOUR
Enacting Strategy Five

In a major crisis, such as a flood, fire, earthquake or a health crisis, you will have opportunities, if you have the resources to supply what is needed during the crisis.

In every crisis there is opportunity. However, in order to prosper, you need to keep abreast of what is going on and what is needed, so you can effectively *'seize the chance to gain advantage'*. In most situations flexibility is required, because you may be asked to design a new product to meet the needs of the post-disaster situation. This can happen in a situation such as following an earthquake, where opportunities present themselves for architects and builders who are required to design something that will withstand another similar disaster.

Key Points when using Strategy Five
- Keep abreast of what is going on in the markets you are in or want to do business in.
- What might be a problem for another business might be an opportunity for you, so be ready to act.
- In situations of crisis, consider what opportunities might exist for your business.

Make a noise in the east and attack in the west *means "to shift the focus from one place by drawing attention to another place"*

In any battle the element of surprise can provide an overwhelming advantage. Even when face to face with an enemy, surprise can still be employed by attacking where he least expects it. To do this you must create an expectation in the enemy's mind, through the use of a feint. The enemy's command becomes confused. Subdue the enemy when it has lost its discipline.

*D*uring the Warring States period Zhu Jun besieged Yuan city. To ensure success, the first move he made was to secretly position half his army out of sight to the west of the city. Zhu Jun then took the rest of his army around to Yuan city's eastern wall, where he launched an attack. Once the people of Yuan city had rushed to defend the eastern wall, Zhu Jun's remaining troops, launched a successful attack from the west, where the city wall was undefended.

When Zhu Jun attacked the eastern wall of Yuan city he applied Strategy Six - **Make a noise in the east and attack in the west** by '*creating an expectation through the use of a* *feint*' and the people of Yuan city thought this was the actual attack. While they were busy defending the eastern wall, Zhu Jun attacked on the western wall of the city, where they '*least expected the attack*'. They '*became confused*', and Zhu Jun was able to attack the city with little resistance from the people.

When you find yourself being distracted from the main point, then you know Strategy Six is in action. The distraction or diversion will generally cause you to lose the focus of your original intention. Once you have lost this focus the strategist then has the upper hand.

Negotiating with Chinese People

EXAMPLE ONE
Strategy Six in action (against you)

If you are an importer of products from China; a likely scenario where Strategy Six may be used against you is where you want to question the high price you are paying for the products you are purchasing. To resolve this, you decide to visit the factory in China to discuss the price issue. In preparation for this meeting you prepare yourself to propose a lower price to your supplier. During the meeting you discuss this price issue with your Chinese contact. When applying this strategy during the meeting your contact will talk about several other things, such as delivery dates and size of orders, and divert the conversation away from the price so you '*become confused*'.

Even when *'face to face with your contact in China'*, you can still be taken off the track when you least expect it. It is often only after you have left their office that you realise you have not discussed what you had planned, which in this case was the price. In this scenario, by using Strategy Six, the person with whom you went to discuss the price gets through the whole meeting without discussing money, as they have diverted the conversation to other product issues.

Example One
Guarding yourself against Strategy Six

This is a strategy to divert you from the main point. Once you are aware Strategy Six is being played out on you, in order to guard yourself against this strategy, it is important to keep reverting back to the main point of your meeting. Ensure the original intention of your meeting is clear and that you are not distracted. This is often an exhausting process.

To prevent yourself from becoming exhausted there are several actions you can take. Come to the negotiation with others in your team who understand Strategy Six, and who will keep reminding you of the main goal of the negotiation such as to get a lower price.

Ensure that you do not let a larger team negotiating on home turf dominate your time and exhaust you. Change the venue. Use your own driver. Find a 'reason' to call your family, even if all you do is rest or plan your next move.

EXAMPLE TWO
Strategy Six in action (against you)

If you are trying to lower the price of the product, your Chinese supplier may surprise you by readily agreeing to your proposed lower price. The ease of achieving your negotiation goal is likely to create some satisfaction in you and make you feel you have achieved the goal of the meeting.

When Strategy Six is applied, *'surprise can occur where you least expect it'*. It might be that part of the deal for your Chinese supplier to accept this low price request is for you to compromise on other things, such as the specifications or the quality of materials. This scenario places you in a position where if you decide you want the lower price, you will need to agree to change the design of your product or use cheaper materials to save costs. It then becomes impossible to save costs if you want to keep the original materials and design of your product.

EXAMPLE TWO
Guarding yourself against Strategy Six

In this scenario it is crucial to have all possible avenues covered, so if Strategy Six is used you are ready to provide your response. You need to carefully plan your response so you achieve what you originally went into the meeting for. Before the meeting, think through all of the possible diversions your Chinese supplier may use when applying

Strategy Six, and decide what you can accept, what you cannot, and what you can trade or change. In this situation, a slight design change to your product may be acceptable, and your product can continue to uphold its high standard even though you agree to use materials of a slightly lesser quality. The most important thing when this strategy is applied is not to over-compromise, as this will be detrimental to your relationship with your Chinese supplier, and you are likely to feel dissatisfied with the end product. If you cannot compromise on anything, it is important to continually keep returning to your reason for the meeting and make sure the discussion does not get taken in another direction. This repetition is sometimes known as the 'Broken Record Technique' in Western communication skills training.

Key Points when Strategy Six is used against you

- Thoroughly prepare for the meeting with your Chinese contact and try to think of all possible diversions that may be applied.
- Keep your meeting on track so that you are not diverted away from the original intention of the meeting.
- Assess what is acceptable for you to compromise on and do not cross that line.

If your Chinese contact or customer is negotiating with you for a lower price, a way of applying Strategy Six is to discuss everything about the product apart from the price. Strategy Six is about diverting attention. You can discuss points such as the exceptional quality and the popularity of the product. If they are the first customers to buy your product, you can explain that they will be the first into the market place and have the possibility of being the leaders in their field. A scenario where Strategy Six is routinely used is in selling real estate. The Chinese customers want to talk about the price and the real estate agent can apply Strategy Six by discussing features of the property such as the location, the size of the rooms, the luxury of the fittings, the proximity to shopping and schools. In other words, anything but the price.

Negotiating in a Western Environment

EXAMPLE FOUR
Enacting Strategy Six

Imagine your company is innovating or shifting direction on an existing product line. To make sure that the information does not get to your competitors you need to divert your competitors' attention away from your new developments until you are ready to launch your product.

Diversions from your new product can be achieved *'through the use of a feint'*, by focusing on other items in your range that are unrelated to this new product. This then distracts your competitors away from what you are really doing, and alleviates your concern about a competitor copying you. By using Strategy Six in this way you can move forward with your new product safely and securely. This gives you the opportunity to be the first to the market with your new idea, because your idea has been protected from being exposed to your competitors.

Key Points when using Strategy Six

- Use distraction from your main goal to prevent others stealing your ideas or beating you to a new market.
- Create diversions to distract your customers from challenging you on price or quality or service.
- When you are being entertained by a supplier, ask yourself what questions they are hoping you will not ask.

Your Next Steps

Having just finished reading *Tame the Tiger*, here are some suggestions for your next steps:

- Now I can plan my approach when I am negotiating in any situation.
- The 36 Strategies will help me when communicating with Chinese people.
- I will share this knowledge with my colleagues.
- I want to read *The Dao of Negotiation* series. I'll find them at **www.leoniemckeon.com**
- I will contact Leonie to:
  - Help me think completely differently about my business development challenges.
  - Deliver a presentation for my next conference or other event.
  - Deliver 36 Strategies workshops to my team.
- Because **Pronounce Mandarin - The Easy Way** is perfect for beginners, I will learn how to correctly pronounce Chinese names and some useful Mandarin Chinese words and phrases via **www.pronouncemandarin.com**

Go to **www.leoniemckeon.com** for more information about the 36 Strategies. Leonie has several informative videos and blogs to help you further your understanding of how to negotiate in any business environment.

WHAT PEOPLE SAY ABOUT WORKING WITH LEONIE MCKEON

BEC HARDY WINES

"I can't tell you how much you have given our family, and me personally, through your insights about the 36 Chinese Strategies. Understanding how the 36 Chinese Strategies are applied in Chinese business culture was the lightbulb moment which has led to such revenue growth, opportunities and personal growth. This has been one of the great, exciting professional and personal journeys and achievements of my life. Thanks again."

Richard Dolan, Joint Managing Director

HATCH, Western Australia

"Anyone who has the pleasure of having dealings with China and the Chinese will find Leonie's 36 Chinese Strategies workshops invaluable. The workshops were eye-opening and had the right amount of humour and personal stories to more than keep our attention."

Denis Pesci, PDG Hub Director, Western Australia

Fletcher Building

"From a personal perspective, Leonie was instrumental to our Chinese cultural program developed for the Super Retail Group. The target audience for the workshop was our Management and Leaders from Logistics, Marketing and Category. In organising the program for the team, I found Leonie incredibly resourceful, totally understood the brief and built value-add to the program. Often you don't know what you don't know so great to have a Subject Matter Expert to guide and shape a very successful program."

Shirley Brown, Capability Development Manager – Australian Distribution

Australian American Fulbright Commission

"The Art of Negotiation – 36 Strategies derived from 'The Art of War' workshop delivered by Leonie at the Australian Institute of Company Directors (AICD) challenged conventional thinking."

Peter de Cure, Chairman, Australian American Fulbright Commission

Kmart

"The training that Leonie provided to our team was excellent. The program was practical, delivered with context, and opened the team members' minds to learning more about how to do better business in China. I have no doubt that what we have learned will be applied and will provide great outcomes for our business. Leonie has also provided a great personal development opportunity for members of our team."

Matthew Webber, International Supply Chain Manager

The Dao of Negotiation
The Path between Eastern Strategies and Western Minds

		Strategy Number
Book One – *Tame the Tiger*	Advantageous Strategies	1, 2, 3, 4, 5, 6
Book Two – *Deceive the Dragon*	Opportunistic Strategies	7, 8, 9, 10, 11, 12,
Book Three – *Lure the Tiger*	Strategies for Attack	13, 14, 15, 16, 17, 18
Book Four – *Bewilder the Dragon*	Confusion Strategies	19, 20, 21, 22, 23, 24
Book Five – *Endure the Tiger*	Strategies for Gaining Ground	25, 26, 27, 28, 29, 30
Book Six – *Flee the Dragon*	Strategies for Desperate Situations	31, 32, 33, 34, 35, 36

The Dao of Negotiation:
The Path between Eastern Strategies and Western Minds

by Leonie McKeon

Leonie McKeon

tame the
tiger

Negotiating from
a position of power

BOOK ONE

Leonie McKeon

deceive the
dragon

Negotiating to
retain power

BOOK TWO

Leonie McKeon

lure the
tiger

Negotiating in
confronting circumstances

BOOK THREE

Leonie McKeon

bewilder the
dragon

Negotiating
amongst confusion

BOOK FOUR

Leonie McKeon

endure the
tiger

Negotiating
to gain ground

BOOK FIVE

Leonie McKeon

flee the
dragon

Negotiating
when all else fails

BOOK SIX

More Control, More Success, More Wins!

Based on *The Art of War*, *The Dao of Negotiation* series unmask the 36 Strategies used in Chinese culture and business.

This incredible series of 6 books provide invaluable tips for any business person looking to improve their overall negotiation skills, as well as become better at negotiating with Chinese People.

Discover how you can use this ancient wisdom for more business success.

www.leoniemckeon.com

www.ingramcontent.com/pod-product-compliance
Lightning Source LLC
Chambersburg PA
CBHW060639210326
41520CB00010B/1667